Inspired

A year's session outlines
for Christian youth groups

Suzi Stock

kevin
mayhew

By the same author,
also published by Kevin Mayhew

What Did Jesus Do?
ID
. . . Yeah And?

First published in 2005 by

KEVIN MAYHEW LTD
Buxhall, Stowmarket, Suffolk, IP14 3BW
E-mail: info@kevinmayhewltd.com
www.kevinmayhew.com

9 8 7 6 5 4 3 2 1 0

ISBN 1 84417 387 9
Catalogue No. 1500790

Edited by Sophia Sorrell
Typeset by Fiona Connell Finch
Cover design by Jonathan Stroulger

Printed and bound in Great Britain

Contents

Introduction

This resource is intended to supply a year's session outlines for Christian youth groups. All the sessions have been tried and tested amongst various groups of young people (uncommitted, new, and 'mature' Christians). The sessions are simple to follow and require minimal preparation. Various songs are suggested throughout the resource (full details of these can be found at the end of this book) but can be replaced with alternative relevant songs. The session plans could easily be built upon for groups who meet for more than an hour but they are also ideal for those who have less time.

Each session plan includes Bible passages and so also provides a basis for talks. Split into 4 sections and enabling various people (even the young people themselves) to lead the group, each session follows a set structure:

- an icebreaker question or challenge
- a time to focus on God
- a chance to explore the key concept or theme
- an opportunity to apply this to everyday life.

The outlines are ideal for cell church groups and most other youth groups. School and college Christian Union leaders may also find them useful.

With 40 outlines, there is more than enough material for a whole year – considering school holiday breaks and social event weeks. The outlines are listed alphabetically by theme and can be run in any order.

Group members will benefit most if they are enabled and equipped to take on some of the responsibilities of leadership by running parts of each session. The outlines are not aimed at a particular age but would cater for all 11-18 year olds, although more established Christians may require additional material. Most youth workers voice the common problem of running out of ideas. My hope in producing this resource is that it will inspire them and their groups.

Suzi Stock

Icons

The following icons are used in each session:

 Icebreaker

 Focusing on God

 Exploring the key theme or concept and the relevant Bible texts

 Concluding thoughts and activities; inspiring the group to apply the inherent message to their everyday life.

1 Actions speak louder

Question: What is the most meaningful action you can think of that someone (friend, family, teacher, etc.) has ever done for you to show how much they love you? (It has to be an action, not something they have said!)

Listen to a song that reflects on the meaning of the Cross (for instance 'The Cross has said it all' by Matt Redman) or watch a video clip of the crucifixion scene. Each pray a simple prayer thanking God for showing his love for us in action through the Cross.

If you were put on trial for being a Christian, would there be enough evidence to convict you? (The attitudes and actions of each person are important in this trial.)
Read **1 John 2:3-6** and **James 2:16, 17**
• **Discuss:** When is it hard to stick to your beliefs? What words about Christianity could be shown in action more (for instance love, helping others, serving the poor, not putting things like drink, relationships or addictions before God)? Make a list.

Get each person to write down a few things they claim to believe but struggle to adhere to in practice. Then encourage the group to think about ways they could help themselves in these areas (for instance to think before speaking, do volunteer work, not put themselves in situations where they will be tempted).

Spend some time in prayer – place these things on or at a cross and listen to a song about surrendering to God, for instance 'Surrender'.

2 Addictions

Game: Chubby bunnies – Two volunteers compete to see how many marshmallows each person can fit in their mouth whilst saying 'addictions' after each one. The more marshmallows in their mouth the harder it gets. It is the same with addictions: as they occupy more space in our lives we have less space for God.

Listen to the song 'Investigate' by Delirious. Discuss the words and say how they apply to you or what they mean to you. Can people honestly pray the words of the song and mean it? Lead the group in prayer, asking that people would see what they rely on in their life instead of God.

Activity: Brainstorm different addictions people can have.
N.B. Anything that takes over our lives can become an addiction. We should strive for balance.
Read **1 Corinthians 6:12, 18-20**
        Ephesians 4:22-24; 5:1,18
        Colossians 2:7,13
* **Discussion:** Do they think that the Bible has too many 'don'ts'?
* How might these guidelines they have read make sense practically as well as spiritually? Is it good advice for all people or just Christians?
Read **2 Corinthians 3:17; 5:17; John 8:31, 32** and **34**
* What does freedom in the Spirit mean?

Invite them to think about their own addictions and to ask God to help them be released from them. If possible write the addictions down on scraps of paper; as a visual at prayer time either burn them or throw them in a bin in the centre of the room. Close in prayer.

3 Alcohol

Challenge: Get hold of various non-alcoholic drinks (such as J2O, non-alcoholic wine, fruit cocktails and so on). Have a tasting test to decide which contain alcohol and then reveal that they're all non-alcoholic. Use this to talk about why people might drink alcohol, why people enjoy it, and when it is detrimental (for instance 'being under the influence', hangovers, violence, drink-driving, reliance and so on).

Brainstorm the advantages and disadvantages of alcohol. Thank God that he gives us the tools to work out what is best for our life and to realise that the Bible is full of words of wisdom that are relevant to our lives today.

In small groups look up the following verses:
> **Proverbs 23:29-35**
> **Ephesians 5:18**
> **Proverbs 20:1**
> **John 2:1-10**

- Discuss the advice given; can they relate to the sense of it? Share personal stories.
- Do they think Christianity is against alcohol? Why did one of Jesus' miracles involve turning water into wine?
- List ways when alcohol is not promoted by Christianity (for instance when it leads to being drunk and when it becomes an addiction).
- Discuss the latest soap drama involving alcohol dependence and what we can learn from it.

Can they commit to God's advice to avoid getting drunk? Pray for those who might find this hard – perhaps because of peer pressure or their own enjoyment of alcohol.

Consider getting hold of some information on alcohol from organisations like HOPE UK and using this with the group if they would like to know more. HOPE UK supply non-alcoholic cocktail recipe leaflets (online: www.hopeuk.org   phone: 020 7928 0848).

4 | *Being a good influence*

Question: Who has influenced you most in your life and why? Which famous people are good influencers? Which famous people could be considered bad influencers? Explain.

On a large piece of paper make a list of all the ways Jesus influenced others – either from specific Bible stories (such as Zacchaeus) or from people's own experiences.

As a group or small groups make up a song or rap thanking God for his influence in the past, present and future.

Ask the group to think of times when they were a bad influence on someone else or when they were influenced to do something bad and then stage a chat show in which they tell the story. Have the rest of the group as the audience, offering their advice and questions. Read **Proverbs 13:20; Matthew 5:13-16**

* Explain that pubs and bars have peanuts available as the salt makes people thirsty, so encouraging people to drink more and making the pub more money!
* Jesus says that we should be like salt for him: making other people thirsty for him.

Hand out peanuts (or a candle to those who are allergic!) and ask them to think about whether they are like salt and light for Jesus. Encourage them to be honest about the things that hold them back from being a Christ-like influence on others. Pray in pairs or as a group. Read **Ephesians 5:1, 2** to close.

5 Boy–girl relationships

Question: What five things are the most important traits of an ideal boyfriend or girlfriend, and why?

Share any nightmare 'first date' stories or 'meet the parents' catastrophes.

Thank God that although the Bible says nothing about dating it does give certain guidelines that can apply to our relationships. List these and thank God for them. Ideas might include: the kind of people we should be, the way we should treat one another, and the way people we are dating should treat their other friends. Finally, discuss why boys and girls go out anyway and the meaning of real love.

In pairs look up the following verses:
- **James 3:17**
- **1 Corinthians 6:18-20**
- **Philippians 2:3, 4**
- **2 Timothy 2:22**
- **Philippians 3:14**
- **1 John 3:18**
- **Hebrews 13:4**
- **James 1:19**
- **1 Corinthians 13:4, 5**

Get the group to discuss how these principles could inform us about God's plan for us within boy–girl relationships.

The Christian principle here is that our lives should reflect the love of Jesus; we shouldn't mess around with people's feelings or lives. Spend some time praying for those who may have issues with this or any of their friends who are struggling with this.

6 *Bride of Christ*

Question: Does anyone know the different symbols for anniversaries (first year – paper, 50th – golden)? See if you can make a complete list prior to the session. Has anyone been to a silver or golden wedding anniversary party or celebration? Why do people celebrate anniversaries?

Question: What do you think idolatry is? Read the second commandment in **Exodus 20:4**. Make a list of examples.

Read **Hosea 1:2-11; 3:1-5**
- Look at the story of Hosea and summarise the story.
- Use any relevant commentaries or books that talk about this story and introduce the idea of humans being like Gomer in the eyes of God, yet he keeps loving us.
- Explain the concept of unconditional love and how this was illustrated through Hosea and Gomer's relationship. Obviously neither Hosea nor God were happy with this unfaithfulness, but Hosea stayed faithful to Gomer and God stays faithful to us.
- Introduce the idea that God sees the Church as his bride, just as Gomer was Hosea's bride (read **Ephesians 5:22-33**).

Play a song that talks about having Jesus as number one in our lives such as 'Jesus, you alone' by Tim Hughes or 'Be the centre'. Pray that we might be more faithful to what we believe.

7 Don't lie or slander

Game: Play the board game Taboo or the 'yes–no' game where questions are put to a volunteer but they cannot answer yes or no and they cannot repeat answers or hesitate for too long.

Get hold of some balloons and pens and invite people to write a prayer of praise on the balloon and tie these somewhere to make a prayer wall of balloons.

Read **James 3:3-10**

- The games played earlier will have illustrated how hard it can be not to say some things. This is true in everyday life and the Bible says we need to control the things we say (read **Colossians 3:8-10; 12-15, 17**).
- The Bible also says that we should be consistent in our lives (we shouldn't praise God one minute and then be nasty to others the next). We need to think carefully about what we say and think each day.
- Explain that we should not excuse the way we speak or the things we say because of our age – the effects of our words can be damaging to others and be hurtful to God.

Play the song 'May the words of my mouth' by Matt Redman and invite people to write a prayer to God listing the areas in their lives that they need to control more. This may include swearing, lying, talking about people behind their backs or being negative.

8 Double life

Question: If you could be anyone else who would you be and why? Perhaps ask for one trivial answer and a more serious one!

Listen to a song about God's consistency, such as 'Yesterday, today and forever' by Vicki Beeching. Thank God that we can rely on him even when our lives change.

Read **John 17:13-19**
- Discuss the meaning of 'to be in the world but not of it'. What does it mean to be 'of the world' (verse 16)?
- How should a Christian be seen by the world? (verses 15, 16)
- What is Jesus' prayer in verse 17?
- 'Sanctify' means to be set apart – to be chosen for God's special purposes. What does it mean to be sanctified by the truth? What is God's purpose for Christians 'being in the world'? Jesus expects his followers to be noticeably different. Do you want to be noticeably different?
- Are you prepared to go against the flow? What might this mean?
- Should we consider 'being in the world but not of it' as leading a double life?

Share any times where friends noticed something different about you. Did you become a Christian because of seeing the difference in a Christian you know? Pray that friends would see Jesus in us and that we would be in the world but behave differently to the world (read **Luke 8:16-18**).

9 Evangelism 1

On a slip of paper ask your group to write down three things about being a Christian that they would say to an alien. Then share stories of when people have told their friends about being a Christian and their responses.

Matchstick testimony: Get some long cooks' matches and in the time it takes for the matchstick to burn invite people to explain why they are a Christian and when they made this commitment. Invite those who aren't Christians to share when they joined the group and why.

Read **Matthew 28:16-20**
- Why should we tell people about Jesus? What should our motives for evangelism be? (Answer: love!)
- Discuss inappropriate ways of telling people about Jesus such as yelling 'hell and damnation' on a street corner!

Read **Matthew 13:3-23**
- This parable can be used to illustrate how people respond to the Word of God in different ways. Discuss what the seed represents and what the ground represents.
- Look at 3 of the responses and share any personal experiences of speaking to people about Jesus, for example:
    1. Seed on hard ground – they harden their heart and don't want to know.
    2. Seed amongst thorns – they listen to what you say but are distracted by the problems and temptations around them.
    3. Seed that fell on good soil – they take in what you say and become Christians, or are interested in doing so.

We should always tell people about Jesus with gentleness and respect. People are rarely converted by shouting and arguments; rather by genuine love, revelation through the Holy Spirit and by seeing the effect Christianity has on our lives. Get the group to write down 3 names of non-Christian friends and to think about what is stopping them from becoming Christians. Pray for them and pray for boldness to be able to share their faith with friends.

10 Evangelism 2

Question: If you were about to die and had just one phone-call to make, who would you phone and why?

Play the song 'I remember the day' by Jeff Searles or another appropriate song that looks back to conversion (for instance 'Oh happy day'). Thank God for 'finding' us and encourage a couple of people to share their testimony.

Read **Luke 15:1-7**
- Are we like the shepherd in verse 6? Do we tell others in excitement of what we have found in God? Why or why not?

Read **Acts 1:8**
- It is our responsibility to tell others what we've found. How is this hard? Share stories of verbally telling people about Jesus.
- Actions speak louder – agree or disagree? How should our lives tell people about what we believe? If an alcoholic says they've given up drink but then you see them with a drink you rightly doubt their words.
- Christianity is all about love. If people do not see love in our lives might they doubt how much a difference God can actually make?
- Share stories where people have commented and been impressed by the way we live our lives differently.

Hand out A4 pieces of paper and get them to write the name and relationship of someone they know who is not a Christian (e.g. Carol, mum or Chris, a friend). Play a song that talks about people being 'found' such as 'Can a nation be saved' by Matt Redman. Spread the papers on the floor and as the music plays each jumps from one paper to another saying a simple prayer for that person out loud or silently.

11 | Faith

Play the trust game – all stand in a tight circle and one person goes in the middle and falls in any direction and trusts the group to catch them. Or pair up and fall back into your partner's arms. Step back slowly and see how far people can trust each other.

Choose a song that really makes you feel close to God, or one that has helped you through a tough time (ask people a week before to bring a song each and play some of these).

Ask people to share a specific incident where they have turned to God when they needed him, or a time when they didn't turn to God but later realised that they should have.

Read **Hebrews 11** (all or parts of it).
- Ask people to share times when they have put faith in something or someone and have been let down, or when they have been right to do so. How easy is it to do this?
- Share things about God that people struggle to believe and why.
- Invite people to make a list of things that cannot be seen but that we know exist (for instance wind – we know it is there because of its effect on trees and other things outside and we can hear it). Then ask people to make a list of how we know God exists (for instance creation, the complicated and clever human mind and body, spiritual experiences and so on).

Read **Matthew 14:25-32**
- People often criticise Peter for his little faith in this story but what about the other disciples who do not even get out of the boat? Who are we most like in this story?

Play 'Can we walk upon the water?' by Matt Redman, or another song about having faith such as 'Can't give up now' by MaryMary. Pray that people would have faith both during the bad times in their lives and the good, and that people would be able to look to the Mountain Maker and not the mountains in their lives (**Matthew 17:20, 21**).

12 | Friends

Game: Choose two volunteers who think they are best or at least quite good friends. Devise a series of questions for one friend to answer on paper about the other. Have the other write down their own answers and then reveal how well the friends know each other! Questions could include: favourite music group, favourite colour, middle name, siblings' names and ages and so on.

Listen to a song about friendship with God such as 'What a Friend I've found' by Delirious? or 'You've got a Friend' by Brand New Heavies or 'What a Friend' by MaryMary.

Read **1 John 4:7-21**
- How can we show our love for people in our friendships? What about people who are not our friends?
- When we are finding it hard to love our friends and neighbours, what can we do and what should we do?
- Encourage people to imagine Jesus in front of their friends and see if that helps them to love as Jesus requests.

Thank God for our friends and pray that he might help us love them more fully and treat them better – even to try and treat them as if they were Jesus (read **Matthew 25:31-45**).

13 Friendship with God

Questions: 1. What makes a good friend?
2. What makes a bad friend?

Share examples of good friends and thank God for these friends.

Read **Luke 10:38-42**
- How does this story tell us that Jesus wants to be friends with us?
- How important is time in friendship? Does it make sense that Jesus also wants our attention and time?

Read **John 15:12-15**
- Do people view God as their friend? Why do or don't they?
- The Bible makes it clear that God is our master but also our friend and that we should fear him, as well as have a friendship with him. This idea is called *friendship and the fear (respect).*
- These two qualities seem worlds apart but an example of this can be seen in a dog and its owner. Some say a dog is a man's best friend but at the same time the dog also respects its master – the dog knows who will feed him, etc.
- Do people feel they view God more as a master than a friend?

Play the song 'Friendship and the fear' by Matt Redman. Encourage people to think about whether their friendship with God is like that described in **John 15:12** or not. Pray that people would recognise God as both friend and master.

14 God – the judge

Play the card game 'Cheat' (for small groups use one pack of cards, for larger groups use multiple packs). Deal out all of the cards. The object of the game is to get rid of all your cards, cheating if you need to. The person who starts can lay face down any card and any number of that card they have. They must say what they are putting down (e.g. three 2s). If anyone in the group has reason to believe that they are cheating they must call out 'cheat' as the person puts down their cards. If they were correct and the player has cheated, the player picks up all the cards from the middle. If they were wrong the challenger must pick up all of the cards. If no challenge is made the next person must lay down card/s either one lower or higher or the same, cheating if necessary!

Share something good that has happened in the week and thank God for these things.

Read **John 8:3-11**
- Ask what they would have done if they were Jesus.
- What does this story tell us about Jesus?
- How did the Pharisees and teachers of the Law feel?
- How would the woman have felt?
- Discuss the saying: 'If you miss the mark by an inch or a mile you still miss the mark.'
- Jesus says that we all sin so who are we to judge others? Only God can judge.
- Why do we often find it easier to judge others rather than support them and stick up for them?

Pray for individuals who know they are often too quick to judge. Share strategies people use to remember to support others and not to judge.

15 | *God wants what's best for you*

Share stories of when you had to stop doing something. At the time it felt as if stopping had ruined your fun but looking back you can see that it was actually the best thing to do.

Look at the Ten Commandments in Exodus 20. Go through each one and think about how each 'rule' makes sense and the possible consequences if they are not adhered to.

Thank God for his rules that are there to protect us, not ruin our fun.

Read **John 10:10** and **Psalm 103:5**
- Being a Christian is not all about rules (do's and don'ts) just for the sake of it. God wants what's best for us and because he created us he knows what's best for us.
- List some examples of where a parent knows better than a child (for instance touching fire – some things are too dangerous for a child to experience by themselves, so a parent would tell them 'no!'; the child might be upset and feel that their fun and excitement had been spoiled).
- Good things are not always what we like or want – but they are good!

Thank God that he has our best interests at heart. Pray that we would dare to live the best life he has for us and that people would notice that we are different.

Perhaps the group members could write prayers in poem or psalm form and read these to the rest of the group.

16 *God's Love*

Question: Discuss the good things we want from a father and the bad things that we don't want.

Listen to 'The Father's song' by Matt Redman and encourage the group to picture God as their heavenly Father who loves them in all the good ways they listed and more.

Read **Zephaniah 3:17** and ask the group to picture God smiling down at them and, on hearing their name, rejoicing with singing!

Thank God for this truth, however hard it may be to accept.

Read **Matthew 7:9-11**

- Because of our bad/imperfect experiences of fathers we can have a false image of God as a Father.
- Imagine that we are looking at God through a window. This window may have had pebbles of imperfect parenting or rocks of abuse thrown at it, so distorting our vision of God – this can stop us ever knowing God as a good Father and it is not what God wants.

Read **Mark 10:13-16**

- We are all children of God and he has time for us; he wants to hold us, comfort us and be our loving Father.

Pray for the group to be able to understand the heavenly Father's love and to receive it.

17 | *Gossip*

Game: Divide into 2 teams to play Pictionary. Have some large sheets of paper and pens. Have some words written down on scraps of paper. Each team selects one person to draw. That person must draw the words so that their team can guess the word. They must not speak at all. The winning team is the one that guesses the most words.

Or play Actionary – as above, but instead of drawing a picture, the word is acted out.

• What's the nicest thing someone has said to you this week?

Go round the group and say something about God that you really appreciate. Turn that into prayer. Share stories of when God has spoken to people through pictures, words of encouragement, etc. Thank God that he speaks to us and wants to encourage us.

Produce a popular gossip magazine and get the young people to choose a few stories that interest them.
• Discuss why we are so interested in others' lives. Do we really know if the stories in these magazines are true? How might we feel if the magazines were printing stories about us?

Read **James 3:1-12**
• Why is it often more difficult to say positive rather than negative things to the people around us?

Read **Proverbs 11:13; 16:28; 26:22**
• Why do we enjoy gossiping about others? (For instance insecurity, pain, jealousy, makes us feel good, nosiness.) What should we do to help us avoid gossiping about others? (For instance don't talk behind their backs; go straight to the person we have a problem with; when others start gossiping either walk away or stand up for the person they are discussing.)

What good things do your friends need to hear from you? Is there anything you need to say sorry for? Pray for God's strength to do this, and for personal healing when we have been the target of gossip. Read **1 Thessalonians 5:11**.

18 Growing up with God

Share your earliest memory of the most embarrassing moment in your life and why.

Listen to a song about turning to God – an example is 'I turn to you' by Melanie C or 'King of this heart' by Matt Redman. Ask people to think about times in their lives when they had problems but kept going and gained from the experience. Thank God for the ways he can bring good out of even the worst situations.

Read the attached poem called 'Buttprints in the sand'.
- **Discussion:** Explain that like a baby who must learn to walk and fend for itself in time, we also have to learn to walk as a Christian and not expect to be spoon-fed by God. We must search for him too.

Read **Song of Songs 3:1-4**
- Do we, like the lover in the story, search for God when he doesn't seem close? Or do we act stubbornly and sit down and do nothing like the poem suggests?
- It is important to have God as King of our hearts even when life is hard.

Play a song about coming through hard times and still praising God, such as 'Shackles' by MaryMary or 'Let everything that has breath' by Matt Redman.

Read **Psalm 136.** Pray that we might be able to recognise God's love and be mature in hard times rather than have a spiritual temper tantrum!

Buttprints in the sand

One night I had a wondrous dream,
one set of footprints there was seen,
the footprints of my precious Lord,
but mine were not along the shore.

But then some strange prints appeared,
and I asked the Lord, 'What have we here?
Those prints are large and round and neat,
but Lord, they are too big for feet.'

'My child,' he said in sombre tones,
'for miles I carried you along,
I challenged you to walk in faith,
but you refused and made me wait.

'You disobeyed, you would not grow,
the walk of faith you would not know.
So I got tired, I got fed up,
and there I dropped you on your butt.

'Because in life, there comes a time,
when one must fight, and one must climb,
when one must rise and take a stand,
or leave one's buttprints in the sand.'

Anon.

19 | *Hope*

Game: Each person writes on a slip of paper their favourite colour and why. Read the papers out and get the group to guess who chose each colour by their reason for liking that colour.

Play a song about hope (Christian or chart song) such as: 'No more rain' by Angie Stone, 'Gonna get better' by Gabrielle or 'Reach for the stars' by S Club 7. If the song is a chart song pick out the words that could relate to God. Thank God for the hope we can have from him.

Read or summarise the story of Noah's Ark **(Genesis 8 & 9)**.
- How do you think God's promise to Noah gave him hope **(Genesis 9:8-17)**?
- What signs (like the rainbow for Noah) do you see that give you hope and courage for the future? Mariah Carey says, 'After every storm a rainbow appears'.
- Share such stories of God bringing you through.
- Discuss the saying: 'Even if you're lying in the gutter, you're still looking up at the stars.'
- Pray for people in the group and situations in the world that seem hopeless.

Do people see hope for their friends and family who aren't Christians? Write down their names on a huge piece of paper or place nightlight candles in a big cross pattern and light the candles as a symbol of hope and a prayer for their salvation.

20 It's hard being a Christian

Have your friends or family ever given you a hard time for being a Christian? How?

Play a song about heaven and our 'prize' such as 'I can only imagine' by Tim Hughes or 'Wake up my soul' by Matt Redman. Thank God for the reality of heaven and eternity that awaits us.

Read **1 Timothy:10-14**
• Who has gone through trials because of being a Christian but has come out triumphant? Becoming a Christian does not mean an easy ride.

Read **2 Corinthians 4:7-18**
• Is the prize of being a Christian greater than the cost?
• Try to get hold of some stories of martyrs (recent and old – there are some good ones in *Jesus Freak* by DC Talk) and read these out.
• Encourage people to think of ways in which we are lucky compared to these Christians. Could we do what they did? Would we like to?

Pray that people would have perspective during trials and that they would persevere (read **Mark 13:11**).

21 Jesus at the centre

Play the chocolate game. You need a dice, a hat, scarf, gloves, a bar of chocolate, knife and fork. Sit in a circle and take it in turns to roll the dice. When someone rolls a 6 they go into the middle, put on the hat, scarf and gloves and eat the chocolate square by square using the knife and fork to cut it up.

Meanwhile the dice continues round the circle; should anyone get a 6 they cut in and take the hat, scarf and gloves from the person in the middle and so on. The game ends when the chocolate runs out!

Have two or three worship songs that focus on Jesus (for instance 'Be the centre') either on CD or get someone to lead the group in song. Have the words ready for those who don't know the songs.

Read **John 4:4-18**
- If Jesus knows everything about us, does that mean he knows everything we need? Discuss.
- What is this living water? What does this story tell us about Jesus?
- Do you think you can hide from Jesus?
- Do you truly believe God will give you all you need (N.B. **need**, not want)? What kind of things do you need?
- Do you think God knows what you need more than you do?

It might be an idea to split into smaller groups to answer these questions and then come back together and share each group's thoughts and reflections.

Read **John 4:29, 39**
Pray for the group as they strive to share God with those who do not know him. It can seem easier to do this if you have a 'radical' story of conversion to tell but every story of conversion is of great importance to God (**Luke 15:10**).

22 | *Joy*

Questions: What have been the happiest moments of your life and why? How did it make you feel at the time? What makes you happy? Does it last long? How did you feel when you became a Christian? Did you experience joy or have any encounter with God?

Write a poem or a psalm to express joy (or the wanting of) in your life. Go round the group and read them out as prayers.

Joy is one of the fruits of the Spirit (**Galatians 5:22, 23**). It's more than just a temporary feeling of happiness or an experience. Joy lasts, even through suffering.

- To gain a greater understanding of the joy God wants to develop in you as a Christian, and why, read:
  Isaiah 12:2-3 (the joy of salvation)
  1 Peter 4:12,13 (supernatural joy during trials)
  Nehemiah 8:10 (the joy of the Lord is our strength)
- Discuss these verses and what they can teach us now.
- Share examples of Christians they know who despite adverse circumstances seem to have a happiness that won't fade.
- How is happiness different to joy? Listen to the song 'Joy' by MaryMary and discuss the words – how easy/hard is it to sing those words and mean it?
- What can we learn from the song?

Pray for each other in the group (maybe one at a time) that people's hearts would be filled with great joy (**Psalm 4:7**). Pray that people around them would notice that joy in them and be drawn to Jesus.

23 *Justice: serving the poor*

Discuss what it means to be poor. In what ways can people be poor – brainstorm ideas (for instance financially, spiritually, physically and so on).

Play some quiet music in the background and have 3 people ready to read the following passages slowly: **Matthew 27:27-44; 45-54; 28:1-10**. Pray out short prayers of thanks. (To set the atmosphere it could be an idea to light some candles and have some pictures of Jesus on the Cross for people to focus on.)

Read **Isaiah 58:6-12**

- The people in the passage would fast (give up food) and pray but God wasn't pleased with just that. What is the kind of fasting he wants in our lives? This means our lives should always be a 'fast' in some way.
- We've given our lives to Jesus and this means doing things that we wouldn't normally do and *not doing* some other things.
- What things could we as a group not do? (For instance 'fast' a trip to the cinema and give the money away to charity.)
- What things could we do to help the poor? (For instance pray more, clear out old clothes and give them to charity shops; sponsor a child in a Third World country; volunteer work at a soup kitchen and so on.)
- Come up with ideas for individuals and as a group. Plan to actually do some of these things.

Listen to the song 'Led to the lost' by Matt Redman and read out the words as a prayer. Read **Isaiah 58:6-12** once more.

24 | *Keeping the peace at home*

Questions: If you could change one thing about your parents, what would it be? If your parents could change one thing about you, what would it be?

All list three good things about their parents and thank God for these qualities – pray that people would think of the good things, not just the bad (although it is much easier to think of the bad!)

Read **Exodus 21:15, 17; Deuteronomy 27:16**
- We don't follow these laws now, but in light of them, how serious and bothered do you think God is about the relationship between parents and children? Discuss.

Read **Colossians 3:20; 1 Peter 5:5,6; John 19:27**
- Why should we honour and respect our parents, and what does the Bible say about it all? (Jesus looked after his mother even when he was on the Cross!)
- Stage a debate/trial. The case is that a young person has disobeyed his parents and his punishment is a ban from attending church activities for a month.
- Get half the group to support the case of the parents and the other half of the group to present a case for the young person, that it is not fair or right.
- Use this to discuss the importance of understanding, considering and respecting (within reason) the 'opposition's' case (i.e. parents).

Encourage people to think back to the question at the start, about what their parents would change about them. Is this something they need to change? How could they begin to respect their parents more? Read **1 Corinthians 13:4-7** and pray that the group would try to show these characteristics of love to their family as well.

25 *Made in the image of God*

Question: If you could change anything about yourself, what would it be and why? If your friends could take on a trait of yours, what would it be and why?

On a large sheet of paper make a list of the group's qualities: encourage people to say at least 3 positive things about themselves and if people are stuck, offer your own ideas/impressions of them. Thank God for making us all so different and for giving us all qualities we can be proud of.

Pick up *The Matrix* **clip about truth and lies** (red and blue pill)
- Use this clip (4min. 24secs.) to illustrate how the world is full of lies that can affect our self-image.
- Come up with some examples of this – one might be that the world says it's important to be good-looking and that if we are liked by the opposite sex we are loved and have value.
- The flip-side of believing this is that if we are not going out with someone we are ugly, useless and unlovable! The devil wants us to believe these lies (**John 8:44**: the father of lies!).
- We can get trapped in this prison of lies – like the matrix – and God wants us to know the truth (read **John 14:6**): he spent time creating us, he gave us a soul and spirit and he loves us. We are works of art.
- The truth is 'I am not only lovable, but loved more than I could ever imagine, by the most amazing person in the universe. I'm beautiful by definition, not because of what other people think.'
- Read **Romans 8:16, 17; Jeremiah 31:3; 1 John 4:10**.

Listen to a relevant song that promotes believing the truth and fighting the daily battle towards a positive self-image. For example, TLC's song 'Unpretty' or 'Dear lie'. Pray for God's help and encouragement as we step out and try to reject the lies.

26 Making your mark

Question: What do you think you are good at and what do you think the person on your right is good at?

Get hold of some paints and card or thick paper. You may like to run this part at the end of the session.

Whilst listening to the song 'Fill us up and send us out' by Matt Redman, encourage people to think about what it might mean for God to 'send them out' and what impression he wants them to leave on the world.

As a sign of commitment to strive to do this get people to place their hands or feet in paint and place a print on their paper or card.

Pray that people would make a positive mark on those around them and then get washed up!

Read **2 Corinthians 4:7-9**
- Discuss how this passage could be encouraging. Share examples of 'ordinary' people (current or biblical) that God has used for his glory.
- God has given us all gifts and abilities that he can use for great things if we let him.
- What do you think God may be asking you to do for him to make a mark in this world?

Read **Matthew 5:14-16**
- Do you think others see God in you? If not, what do they see?
- Share ways in which we can hide our light and the possible consequences of this.

Pray that we would not hide the light we have found but live unashamed of God and the difference he has made in our lives. Pray for anyone who feels that they know what God would like them to do – commit to support each other in the group.

27 | *Not ashamed of God*

Question: If someone put a gun to your head and asked you to deny Christ or die what do you think you would do? What would you like to do?

Spend some time talking about what it might be like to live in a country or culture where events like this are a reality. Share true stories of martyrs past and present. A good resource for this is *Jesus Freaks* by DC Talk and *The Voice of the Martyrs* (ISBN: 0-86347-388-1 published by Eagle).

Play 'I'm not ashamed of the Gospel' by Delirious? Discuss the words and how true they are or not.

Share examples of when people might be ashamed of God and what might cause them to feel ashamed. Discuss how God might feel when we are ashamed of him.

Thank God that he still sticks by us even when we reject him; pray for the words of the song to be more evident in our lives.

Read one of the 'lost' parables in **Luke 15**

• Write a modern-day version of the parable or produce a play. This could be done in smaller groups and performed or read out in the session.

• Share personal stories/testimonies of standing up for God. Read **Hebrews 11:32-37; 12:1, 2**.

Use page 315 of *Jesus Freaks* to come up with a statement and devise a commitment prayer to be unashamed of the gospel. You may like to hand out copies and get people to sign them as a visual commitment to the prayer and the challenge of being a 'Jesus freak'. Close in prayer.

28 Patience

Question: Have you ever had to wait for something special (e.g. a holiday or present)? How did you feel during the 'waiting time'?

How did you feel when you received it or achieved it? Did you appreciate it more? Did you learn anything along the way?

Challenge: Give everyone a Malteser (or similar sweet) and see who can keep the sweet (not swallow it) in their mouth the longest!

If possible get hold of some flower bulbs and some small flowerpots. Explain that just as bulbs grow roots underground before the flowers grow above the ground, there is often a lot of behind-the-scenes work in our lives that we don't appreciate.

It is easy to get impatient or frustrated at God but we must remember that he sees the bigger picture (he sees below the ground as well) and his perspective is greater than ours.

Get everyone to plant a bulb or plant one bulb collectively as an act of worship. Pray that we would all be open to God working on our roots – not just our flowers!

Read a summary of **Exodus**
- What did God promise Moses and the children of Israel? (see **Exodus 3:7, 8**).
- After delivering the people from slavery in Egypt where did God lead them and why? (**Exodus 13:17, 18**).
- How did the children of Exodus respond? (**Hebrews 3:7-19**).
- How did God respond?

In our modern quick fix, 'I want it now', 'fast food' society, we tend to be only interested in getting what we want, achieving our dreams as quickly as possible, and at any cost.

God is often more interested in the journey than the final destination. We need to be patient as this produces character, hope and faith. It also allows God to refine us along the way.

When we are in a situation where patience is required, we have a choice to trust God (allow him to develop our faith and character) or we can choose rebellion and sin and 'doing it our way'. Read **Romans 5:3-5** (about persevering through trials). Pray.

29 | *Peace*

Activity: Rank these in order of greatest value (1-7) in your life on a piece of paper: money, power, love, fame, peace, friends and family, and a career.

How important is peace? Do people search for peace? How do people find peace and in what things (music, drink, drugs, holidays, sleep)?

Share times when people have felt peace – perhaps in difficult or anxious times. Discuss why or when people might need peace (bereavement, anxiety about their future). Listen to the song 'Peace' by The World Wide Message Tribe.

Get people to lie down or get comfy and shut their eyes – maybe add some atmosphere with dimmed lighting and candles. Pray.

Read **John 14:25-27; Philippians 4:4-7**
- **Discuss:** Do you think God's peace is the same as the world offers?
- What is God's peace for? Do we often mistake peace with everything being problem free?
- Can people feel peaceful amidst suffering?
- What obstacles can we create to prevent us knowing peace?
- Discuss the phrase: Sometimes God calms the storm, sometimes he calms his child. How is peace evident but different in these two situations?

If possible send people off on their own – outside or to a space in the room/s with a lit nightlight candle. Encourage them to sit still on their own, focusing on the candle and blocking out any distractions.

Do this for 5 minutes before coming back together and closing in prayer. Encourage people to spend time this week just 'being' with God and resting with him despite the struggles that they may be facing.

30 Proud to be young

Question: What is your most embarrassing childhood story? Or what did you believe when you were a child that you now laugh about?

Challenge: Get baby photos of the leaders (or even the whole group) and get people to guess who's who!
Have a prize for the person who guesses the most!

Share something good about the past week and something you did differently as a result of last week's session. Thank God for his involvement in our lives.

Read **Luke 2:41-52**
- **Discuss:** Age did not hinder Jesus is his mission – some people might have been doubtful of his knowledge but he did not let that deflate his confidence in the truth.
- How does being young often pose problems today?

Read **1 Timothy 4:12**
- Break this verse down and discuss how we can set an example in our speech, life (conduct), love, faith and purity.
- Some people say that it is understandable why so many young people live wayward lives if we look at their adult role models.
- Is this a plausible excuse or can we see the benefits of reversing the expected and being role models to the adults in our lives?
- What obstacles might we face and should this stop us? Would it stop Jesus?
- Discuss the saying 'to lead an orchestra you need your back to the audience'.

Brainstorm ways that we can set an example to our friends, our family and the church. Pray that we would want to do this and live by example – to be 'little Christs'. Pray that we would be able to do this in all settings and not just the 'easy' places!

31 | *Purity*

Question: What is the hardest part about guy–girl (dating) relationships for you and why?

Challenge: Divide the group into teams and have a race against time to come up with the longest list of things that can be pure (for instance pure orange juice, pure-bred racehorses and so on).
    Have a prize for the team who comes up with the most.

Have each person say and explain what their favourite praise/worship song is and explain why – they may like to share a line or two of the song. Turn this into prayer.

Read **Mark 8:34**
- Discuss how this verse might be used to talk about surrendering our lives to Jesus in the area of sexual purity.

Read **1 Thessalonians 4:2-8**
- Try to get hold of the Message Bible and read this passage from this version as well. Discuss what sexual immorality is (intimacy or sex with someone you're not married to).
- Discuss the meaning of sanctification (to be set apart for a special purpose).
- Break down each verse of this passage and discuss its meaning and application.
- Verse 6 looks at the idea of not 'defrauding' or cheating your brother or sister. Think about the meaning of this (for instance misleading the opposite sex by flirting, playing with their mind or emotions, confusing and pressurising them to go against their beliefs).
- The fact that God has called us to reject impurity and choose sanctification may affect our sexual behaviour – how?
- What happens if we fail God's standards in this area?
- Why does God give us these guidelines? Do you think your life measures up to God's guidelines?

Listen to the song 'Search me, O God' and then split into small groups to pray about the issue of purity. Commit to being accountable to each other in this area.

32 | *Seeking righteousness*

Question: What is the nicest thing someone has ever done for you?

We remember when people do things for us. Are there things that we could do for others to serve them or just make their day? Do we need to change our attitudes?

How often do we put other people before ourselves?

In what ways has God changed you since you became a Christian? Is he changing you at the moment in any way? Thank him now for this.

Get hold of some disclosing tablets from a pharmacy and give every-one a tablet to suck. Explain that dentists use these to show how much plaque is on people's teeth – regular brushing removes plaque. (N.B. You may like to tell the group to bring their toothbrushes to this session to save embarrassment afterwards!)

- Explain that just as none of us like having dirty teeth we should also seek to have clean, pure lives.
- Holiness is about letting God transform our minds, our words, our actions, our thoughts, our hearts – our entire lives.
- We need to truly give every aspect of our lives to him – parts where we fear and sin the most are the parts we haven't fully given to God.
- God may at times draw our attention to areas of our lives that need 'cleaning up'.
- Get a big piece of paper and all write or draw things that get in the way of us having holy lives (Reflect on **Hebrews 12:1, 2**).

Whilst reflecting on the things written on the sheet and the passage from Hebrews, listen to the song 'Create in me a pure heart'. Get people to shut their eyes and listen to the words. Pray for help and encouragement in our attempts to live holy, righteous lives (read **1 Peter 1:13-16**).

33 Starting over

What do you think makes someone a Christian? Discuss.

Whilst listening to the song 'Lord I am not my own' (What I have vowed) by Matt Redman, encourage people to offer silent prayers of repentance to God for wrong things they have said, done or thought in the week.

Read **Mark 8:34-36**
- Discuss this passage and what 'taking up your cross' actually means in day-to-day living. Is it easy?
- Have a general discussion or debate addressing the members' main queries, questions or disagreements with the Christian faith. The leader should try to hold this discussion together without dismissing any issues or trying to get everyone to have the exact same beliefs or understanding of a topic. (This time should be used to gauge where the group are at and could be useful in planning future group topics.)

Get hold of the words and music of the song 'I give you my life' by The World Wide Message Tribe (now known as The Tribe). Hand out the words and read them out loud together as a prayer of re-commitment to God. Then listen to the song and close in prayer.

Do stress that recommitment is a good thing to do (even daily!) because we all mess up and must acknowledge this and so give control of our lives back to God again and again. Becoming a Christian isn't a one-off commitment – it's a daily decision and a daily battle.

34 | *Talents*

Question: What are your talents? What talent would you like to have?

Challenge: Freak or unique?! Ask people to share any strange talents (for instance double-jointed tricks, ear wiggling and so on) and have a prize for the 'freakiest'!

Encourage everyone to think of one talent they have (some people may need help with this) and go round the group, each saying a simple prayer of thanks like: 'Thank you God for giving me the talent of . . .'

Read **Matthew 25:14-28**
- Relate this story to the idea of the talents God has given each of us – how might we be like the servant who hides the master's money? How might we be like the servant who uses his money to raise more? Is not using our own gifts and talents like not opening a Christmas present?
- Get hold of some simple presents (maybe some small cards with Christian prayers on or Christian bracelets, or make something special) and wrap these up.
- Give each member a present and ask them to imagine that this present represents the talents God has given them. He wants us to open this gift and use the talent for its purpose. What use is a bike if it is not ridden? What use is a pet if it is not cared for? What use are our talents if we do not use them?
- We may not think we are good enough or may see others who are better than us and feel worthless, but God has given us talents because he knows that we can use them to benefit us and others and give glory to God (read **Colossians 3:23**).

Listen to the song 'All or nothing' by Athena Cage or 'Dreams' by Gabrielle. Get people to write down on a slip of paper a talent they know they have and that they want to use more for God – and a few ideas of how they might do this. Share in small groups and pray for each other.

35 The Armour of God

Questions: Have you ever been in a fight? How did you protect yourself during the fight? How do you cope in conflict? Do you often find yourself in the midst of conflict? What role do you tend to play (for instance arguer, mediator, victim)?

How would you like to deal with conflict? Do you think conflict can be positive?

Each write a psalm to God. You may like to look at a couple of examples of psalms in the Bible about conflict or hard times. Use the format 'Lord I feel . . . But I know . . . So I will . . .' They should be totally honest to God about how they feel (however irrational) but then take into consideration what they know about the character of God, his intervention in the past, and arrive at something more positive than their initial feelings.

If people are comfortable with doing so, say these psalms out loud as prayers. Listen to the song 'How lovely is your dwelling place' by Matt Redman and pray that we would find sanctuary with God. (read **Psalm 91:1-4**).

Read **Ephesians 6:10-20**
- Break this passage down verse by verse and discuss what it means. It might be an idea to draw a suit of armour to visualise the passage and relate the parts of the suit to the tool kit God has given us to cope with life. Look at how many parts of the armour are used for defensive purposes and how many for attacking.
- **Discuss:** Do people agree that our real battle is with spiritual things? Why or why not?
- Have people had real encounters with negative spiritual things?
- Has being a Christian helped?

Read **Luke 4 :1-13**
- Discuss how Jesus used his tool kit (armour of God) to reject Satan's accusations and temptations. How might we also be more equipped to deal with difficult times? (For instance knowing the Bible better, praying more, being accountable to Christian friends.)

Listen to a song about relying on God such as 'Shaken up' by Delirious? or 'When my heart runs dry' by Matt Redman and pray for God's protection in times of spiritual battle. It might be an idea to mime putting on the armour of God as a prayer.

36 The Bible

Ask each person to choose a verse from the Bible that has meant a lot to them and explain why.

Choose a song that talks about the importance of reading the Bible (for instance 'Eat the Word' by The World Wide Message Tribe). Read the lyrics out and then listen to the song. Share how you feel about the lyrics – are they true? Do you want them to be true? Pray for people wanting the words to become reality.

Read **2 Timothy 3:10-17**
- **Discuss**: How did Timothy learn? What do verses 15 and 16 say the Bible is good for?

Read **Psalm 119:97-112**
- Is this your attitude to the Word of God? Ask people about the last time their life changed because of something they read in the Bible.
- Share how people find reading the Bible – discuss ways to help (for instance Bible-reading notes, reading with a friend, Youth Bible that has life-help sections).
- Try to get hold of some Bible-reading notes for the group. UCB produce a free booklet called *Word for Today* and they now have a youth edition (phone: 01782 642100 for more information).

Read **2 Timothy 4:5b** – this says we should tell people the Good News. The Bible is often called The Good News and 'Gospel' (the name given to the first four books of the New Testament) means Good News.

Pray that people would be able to know more of the Bible and be able to tell the Good News to friends who aren't Christians yet. Pray for those friends.

37 The Body of Christ

Game: Get into groups of 3 and have a 'make a banana sandwich' competition. Persons 1 and 2 are blindfolded – person 1 puts their hands through person 2's arms and becomes their hands. Person 3 can see and must guide the other two in making a sandwich and person 1 (the hands) must successfully feed the sandwich to person 2.

Get each person to think of two people who have really helped them grow as a Christian – go round thanking God for these people.

Read **1 Corinthians 12:12-31**: The Body of Christ.
- On a large piece of paper draw a body and ask people to relate the different parts of the body to different gifts or qualities people can have (for instance hands = helper; ears = listener and so on).
- Share times when people have had broken limbs or had some other injury and how it affected their life. Same with the church – it needs all its parts or it won't function properly.
- Show an illustration of the appendix – no one is totally sure of its function in the human body but we know that if it is not healthy it affects the whole body drastically (appendicitis).
- We may feel useless as part of the Body of Christ but we are still important despite not knowing our function *yet*.

Give everyone a piece of paper and get them to write their name on the top – pass these round the group so each member has the chance to write on everyone's paper stating what gifts they see in that person (try to avoid trivial things).

Discuss how we could use these gifts in the group more (for instance someone might be really gifted at listening or praying or leading or acting and these gifts could be used more in future sessions). Close with a prayer.

38 | *The future*

Question: What have you always wanted to do but haven't had the chance? (Choose one 'crazy' thing and one more serious)

Listen to the song 'I can only imagine' by Tim Hughes and turn this into a prayer of trust in God for our future. Play the trust game where everyone stands in a tight circle and each person takes a turn to stand in the middle with their eyes closed and falls back, forwards or sideways into the arms of the group – see who can trust the others the most. Anyone who peeks or shuffles about is disqualified!

Read **Jeremiah 29:11-13**
• Invite people to spend some time in silent reflection and prayer about God taking care of their future.

Read **Matthew 6:25-34**
• Encourage people to share any worries they have about their future and also any dreams, visions and hopes they hold for their life.
• Spend some time talking about these and praying for each other.

Read **Revelation 21** (try to use a modern translation like The Message). Encourage people to catch this glimpse of heaven God has given us and to realise that they are going to be there! Pray for friends and family who do not know God yet.

39 | *What you do to others, you do to God*

Challenge: In pairs blindfold one and get the other to describe a picture without saying what it is (you will need to suggest one – for instance a house); the one who is blindfolded try to draw it (for example: draw a big square with a triangle at the top and so on). Have a prize for the best teamwork.

Listen to the song 'Everything I do, I do it for you' by Bryan Adams or something with a similar message. Encourage people to relate the song to their walk with God and lead into prayer asking God to help this be reality.

Create a talk based on the themes within the following passages: **Matthew 25:35-46; 22:37-40; Luke 6:27-36.**
- Emphasise that loving God means that we must love others; that he commands us to love others and that loving our enemies is the real challenge!
- It is easy to love those we like! If anyone is to love those who do wrong or who are rejected by others, shouldn't it be the Church?
- Imagine that Jesus is there physically in your daily situations – this would probably stop us being out of order or unloving towards people. Discuss any aspects of this that people struggle with.

In threes share how people are in this area and pray for each person in the group. Then pray for those absent from the group, for families, friends and enemies.

40 Worship and praise

Questions: What type of music do you listen to and why? How does it make you feel? What is your favourite worship song or songs that make you think about God the most? (it needn't be a Christian song.)

The leader should bring in a song or two that help them in their worship to play to the rest of the group – it might be an idea to choose a Christian song and a non-Christian song that can both be related to God.

Share with the group the reasons for choosing these songs and what it means to them.

Read **Romans 12:1**
- **Discuss:** What is a sacrifice? How do we sacrifice our lives to God?

Read **Ephesians 5:15-21**
- What kind of music do you listen to?
- What are their themes?
- Are these themes helpful?
- The passage from Ephesians talks about the importance of singing and making music to God. It also talks about how we live our lives. Why is worship not just about singing, but also about our lifestyle?

Read **Philippians 4:8**
- How do the songs you listen to match up to this verse? Worship is more than singing songs – it is about a lifestyle and making a sacrifice of praise (even when we don't want to).
- Listen to the song 'Let everything that has breath' by Matt Redman and pray that each of us would be able to praise God, whatever the weather!

Listen to the song 'Heart of worship' (When the music fades) by Matt Redman. Once we make the effort to praise God we will often sense his presence and our spirits may feel lifted. Close with a prayer.

Details of songs and albums used in this resource

1 The Cross has said it all, *The Songs of Matt Redman*, Kingsway music KMCD2441

2 Surrender, *Surrender*, Vineyard Music 1995022

3 Investigate, *Glo*, Furious? Records

4 Jesus, you alone, *Led to the Lost* or *Heart of Worship*, Survivor Records

5 Be the centre, *Hungry*, Vineyard 1995012

6 May the words of my mouth, *Soul Survivor*, Survivor Records SURCD045

7 Yesterday, today and forever, *Soul Survivor Live 2003*, Survivor Records SURCD5005

8 I remember the day, *Soul Survivor Live 1995*, ICC music ICCD14430

9 Can a nation be saved, *The Songs of Matt Redman*, Kingsway music KMCD2441

10 Can we walk upon the water, *Friendship and the Fear*, Survivor Records SURCD 001

11 Can't give up now, *Thankful*, Columbia label by Sony music COL4979852

12 What a friend I've found, *King of Fools*, Furious? Records

13 You've got a friend. Single: Screen Gems/EMI 570013-2

14 What a friend, *Thankful*, Columbia label by Sony music COL4979852

15 Friendship and the fear, *Friendship and the Fear*, Survivor Records SURCD 001

16 The father's song, *The Songs of Matt Redman*, Kingsway music KMCD2441

17 I turn to you. Single: Virgin Music VSCDT1772 (also on *Northern Star* album)

18 King of this heart, *Father's Song*, Survivor Records SURCD038

19 Shackles, *Thankful*, Columbia label by Sony music COL4979852

20 Gonna get better, *Rise*, Go Beat Records 07314547768-2 (0)

21 No more rain, *Black Diamond*, Arista Records 74321-72775-2

22 Reach for the stars, *Reach*, Polydor Records

23 I can only imagine, *Soul Survivor Live 2003*, Survivor records SURCD5005

24 Wake up my soul, *The Songs of Matt Redman*, Kingsway music KMCD2441

25 Joy, *Thankful*, Columbia label by Sony music COL4979852

26 Led to the lost, *Led to the Lost*, Survivor Records

27 Unpretty and Dear Lie, *Fanmail*, Arista Records 73008260552

28 Fill us up and send us out, *The Songs of Matt Redman*, Kingsway music KMCD2441

29 I'm not ashamed of the gospel, *Cutting Edge 3 & 4*, Furious? Records CE3-4CD

30 Peace, *Chilled*, Alliance Music 1908292

31 Search me O God, *Soul Survivor People's Album*, SURCD009

32 Create in me a pure heart, *Soul Survivor People's Album*, SURCD009

33 Lord I am not my own, *The Songs of Matt Redman*, Kingsway music KMCD2441

34 I give you my life, *Frantik*, Alliance Music 1908142

35 All or nothing, *Save the Last Dance*, Hollywood Records 0927-42431-2

36 Dreams can come true, *Dreams Greatest Hits Vol 1*, Go Beat Records 589374-2

37 Shaken up, *Cutting Edge 3 & 4*, Furious? Records CE3-4CD

38 When my heart runs dry, *Soul Survivor Live 2001*, Survivor Records SURCD060

39 How lovely is your dwelling place, *The Songs of Matt Redman*, Kingsway music KMCD2441

40 Eat the word, *Frantik*, Alliance Music 1908142

41 Let everything that has breath, *The songs of Matt Redman*, Kingsway music KMCD2441

42 Heart of worship, *The Songs of Matt Redman*, Kingsway music KMCD2441

43 I can only imagine, *Soul Survivor Live 2003*, Survivor records SURCD5005

233721